Dare to Dream

Four True Life Stories About
IMAGINATION

COVER ILLUSTRATION:

Justin Ray Thompson

PHOTO CREDITS:

AP/Wide World—Bill Janscha, pp. 8-9, 10; Burt Steel, p. 14; John
Suchocki/*Springfield Union-News*, p. 16; Jay Sailors, p. 21; Scott
Applewhite, p. 22; others: pp. 12, 18 (The Wall)
Hulton|Archive—end pages (Theodor Seuss Geisel) & p. 6
Granger Collection—pp. 24, 26, 24, 26, 27, 28
Sygma—Les Stone, p. 18 (Maya Lin)

Incorporated

Visit us at *www.kidsbooks.com*

VALUES IN ACTION™

Dare to Dream

Four True Life Stories About
IMAGINATION

Imagination is the ability to form a mental picture of something that isn't real or is beyond reach. In this book, you will meet four extraordinary people who dared to dream. They used their imagination to turn dreams into reality, and won admiration and respect for enriching the lives of others.

Amanda Dunbar
by Denise Rinaldo

Theodor Seuss Geisel
by Susan E. Edgar

Maya Lin
by Kathleen J. Edgar

Leonardo da Vinci
by Denise Rinaldo

Amanda Dunbar

born 1982

Like most kids, Amanda Dunbar enjoyed playing with paints and crayons in early-school arts and crafts. Unlike most kids who grow into artists, however, she didn't spend time sketching people and things around her or drawing designs or doodles out of her imagination. Her first real attempt at painting was at age 13, when she signed up for an after-school art class.

Ever since that day in 1996, Amanda has been painting. Viewers are astonished by the grace and skill of her works of art, which now sell for thousands of dollars each. However, it isn't ideas of wealth or fame that keep sending Amanda Dunbar back to her studio. "My inspiration," she says, "comes from creating art that serves humanity, not itself." She uses her gift to support charities and other good causes, including a monument to youths who died by violence committed by other young people.

A Life-changing Gift

Amanda Dunbar—known to her family and friends as Mandi—was born on December 17, 1982, in Thunder Bay, Ontario, Canada. Her father, Ken Dunbar, was studying electrical engineering and her mother, Judi Dunbar, worked as a nurse. It wasn't all technology and science in the Dunbar household, however. Judi Dunbar sometimes worked part-time as an interior designer.

In 1995, the family—Ken, Judi, Amanda, and Amanda's younger sister, Meaghan—moved from Thunder Bay to Allen, Texas, near Dallas. But the biggest change in Amanda Dunbar's young life came a couple of years later, as eighth grade was coming to an end. "I just went to the after-school class for a place to hang out," Amanda said later. It turned out to be much more than that.

At the first class, the teacher invited the students to paint whatever they liked, however they liked. Amanda didn't worry about what to do, she just got started. "I was just having fun," she said. In Amanda's first paintings, however, her teacher recognized an extraordinary ability. "We have to talk to your parents," he told her.

Painting is not easy. It takes most people years to develop a painter's eye. They have to learn how to blend and use colors. They learn composition—what to put on the canvas, and where and how. They study other artists' work and imitate their styles until they develop a style of their own.

"If you are given a gift, you have a responsibility to do something good and positive with it."
—Amanda Dunbar

Amanda Dunbar with Columbine, *one of her paintings commemorating lives lost at a 1999 high school shooting incident*

Amanda, however, seemed to leapfrog right into the sort of work it takes most people years to accomplish.

Amanda can't explain her talent, but she appreciates it as a great gift—from the angels, she says. "I'm just the hand that moves the brush," Amanda tells people. "The canvas and colors tell me where they want to go."

Amanda doesn't use live models—she pictures people and scenes in her head, then paints them. She says that she lets the work flow through her. "I don't think to myself, 'Oh, I need some red here or some blue there.' I just get real quiet inside. . . . The part of my brain that worries shuts off."

"Free Your Mind"

Amanda isn't the only artist in the Dunbar family. Her sister Meaghan, younger by 15 months, is another.

Amanda's gifts of imagination and craft are expressed through painting; Meaghan's, through music. Meaghan sings and plays piano, flute, and piccolo. She hopes to learn how to play the guitar. She also writes songs.

Meaghan sounds a lot like her sister when it comes to talking about how she goes about doing what she does. "You're not even thinking anymore [when performing]," Meaghan says, "you just free your mind and express [yourself]. There's nothing calculated. I don't play the piano, the piano plays me."

Amanda Dunbar with Bubblemaker 2

Giving Something Back

Amanda's artwork caught the eye of Ben Valenty, a noted book publisher and talent scout. Many more people saw her work when her book, *Guided by Angels*, was published in 2000. Amanda also appeared on TV programs, including the popular *Oprah Winfrey* show. The teen was on her way to fame and fortune, but she believed that her gifts had a more important purpose. She started using her work to raise money for good causes.

Amanda's favorite subject to paint is families, especially mothers and children. "Children are our future and they are so important to me," she says. "Through working on . . . [my painting] the thought occurred to me that I could begin a charitable fund using my art." Amanda began donating, selling, and exhibiting her work to raise funds for good causes, especially those whose main goal is helping youth and families.

In 2000, the young artist started Amanda's Angel Alliance. Among the various projects the foundation supports is a monument in California's Mojave Desert. Amanda envisions it as "a symbol of healing and hope"—a 60-foot-tall pyramid, with five sides, painted by her. She hopes that it will remind viewers that youth-on-youth violence is a tragedy and a waste, and will inspire them to seek ways to end it.

Amanda Dunbar can imagine a better world, and is using her gifts to help make it so. "If one person understands the message [in my paintings] or decides to spend time with their children or family," she says, "my work has been successful."

Life Lines

1982 Amanda Dunbar is born in Thunder Bay, Ontario, Canada, on December 17.

1994 The Dunbar family moves to Allen, Texas.

1996 Amanda takes her first art class and shows immediate skill as a painter.

1998 Ben Valenty, a publisher and art-talent scout, sees Amanda's paintings and starts promoting her work.

1999 Amanda meets singer Charlotte Church; the two soon begin doing joint charity projects.

2000 Amanda begins planning the Anthem for Alliance Monument, a five-sided pyramid painted in memory of youths who have died by violence at the hands of other young people.

Theodor Geisel (Dr. Seuss)

born 1904 • died 1991

As a boy, Theodor Geisel *(GUYS-el)* dreamed of becoming a writer. Little did he realize that he would become the best-selling author of children's books worldwide. "Theodor who?" you may say. Most people know him by his other name: Dr. Seuss. Using tongue-twisters, nonsense words, and wacky characters, he has delighted countless readers with his stories about the Grinch and Little Cindy-Lou Who, Sally Spingel Spungel Sporn, Conrad Cornelius O'Donald O'Dell, Snorter McPhail and His Snore-a-Snort Band, Miss Fuddle-dee-Duddle, Thing-a-ma-Jiggers, Hinkel-Horn Honkers, and the Cat in the Hat. A creative genius, Theodor knew how to tell amusing stories to his readers, young and old alike.

Dr. Seuss Is Born

Theodor Seuss Geisel was born in Springfield, Massachusetts, on March 2, 1904. Following his dream to be a writer, he studied English literature in college and trained in the use of proper English. What later made him famous was his ability to make "proper" English fun. He used rhyme and his imagination to make up silly but expressive words, such as *snarggled*, *miff-muffered moof*, and *smogulous*.

In college, Theodor also gained experience as an illustrator for the student newspaper. After college, he began his professional career by drawing comic strips and writing amusing articles, often of a political nature, for newspapers and magazines.

In 1936, Theodor took a trip aboard a train. As he listened to the rhythm of the train moving along the track—clackity-clack, clackity-clack—his quick wit and wild imagination sparked an idea. Putting pen to paper, he wrote a story, in rhyme, about wonderful things he had witnessed while standing on a main street in his hometown of Springfield. He took real items and events and changed them to suit his imagination. Many of the gadgets described in the story were modeled after products manufactured in Springfield's factories. After being rejected by more than 20 publishers, *And to Think That I Saw It on Mulberry Street*, by "Dr. Seuss," was published the following year. Theodor sometimes published under his real name—Theodor Seuss Geisel or Ted Geisel—but he also used pen names, such as Theo LeSieg (*Geisel* spelled backward) as well as the now-famous Dr. Seuss.

Theodor Seuss Geisel greets his most famous creation, the Cat in the Hat.

Teaching Tots

In addition to writing books, Theodor did some work in movies. During World War II, he served in the U.S. Army and assisted film-maker Frank Capra in making documentaries about the war. (Capra's most famous film is probably *It's a Wonderful Life*, often shown on TV at Christmastime.) Awarded the Legion of Merit from the U.S. Army, Theodor also received two 1947 Academy Awards (Oscars) for his documentaries *Hitler Lives* and *Design for Death*. He received another Oscar in 1951 for *Gerald McBoing Boing*, an animated film.

Then Theodor was met with a new challenge. In 1954, *Life* magazine ran a story about illiteracy (the inability to read and write) among young children. The article said that children did not read well because the books they learned from were boring. The author jokingly commented that kids might learn to read more quickly if they were taught using the gibberish of writers like Dr. Seuss. By that time, "Dr. Seuss" had published 10 children's books.

When an editor gave Theodor a list of 225 words used to teach children to read, he let his imagination run wild. The result was *The Cat in the Hat*, published in 1957. Using rhyme and a zany story line as well as 220 of the key words, Theodor created a learn-to-read book that was fun. "A person's a person, no matter how small," he once said about writing for kids. "Children want the same things we [adults] want: to laugh, to be challenged, to be entertained and delighted." Today, many Dr. Seuss books—including *Horton Hears a Who*, *Green Eggs and Ham*, and *One Fish Two Fish Red Fish Blue Fish*—are used to help young children learn the basics of reading.

Some of Theodor's books deal with social issues as well. Among his stories with a message are *The Lorax*, which teaches about the environment; "The Sneetches," which looks at prejudice; and *The Butter Battle Book*, a takeoff on the nuclear-arms race.

During Theodor's lifetime, he sold more than 100 million books, and 17 Dr. Seuss titles are among the top 100 best-selling children's books of all time in the U.S. Count in all his books sold overseas, including those translated into other languages, and Dr. Seuss may be the most-beloved children's author ever. In all, he published 44 children's books and made numerous TV shows and films. In 1984, he

Audrey Geisel, Theodor's widow, with the stamp issued in his honor in 1999

won a Pulitzer Prize—a great honor—for his "special contribution . . . to the education and enjoyment of America's children and their parents."

Theodor Seuss Geisel died in La Jolla, California, on September 24, 1991, but his work lives on, delighting new generations of children and parents the world over.

> *"I like nonsense, it wakes up the brain cells. Fantasy is a necessary ingredient in living; it's a way of looking at life through the wrong end of a telescope. Which is what I do, and that enables you to laugh at life's realities."*
> —Theodor Seuss Geisel

Life Lines

1904   Theodor Seuss Geisel is born in Springfield, Massachusetts, on March 2.

1937   *And to Think That I Saw It on Mulberry Street*, the first book by "Dr. Seuss," is published.

1957   In response to a challenge, Theodor publishes *The Cat in the Hat*, the first of his children's readers. It is a major success. The following year, he founds Beginner Books, Inc.

1984   Theodor receives a special Pulitzer Prize for his lifelong dedication to the education of children.

1991   Theodor Seuss Geisel, author and illustrator of 44 books, dies in La Jolla, California, on September 24.

2002   A national memorial dedicated to Dr. Seuss is scheduled to be unveiled in Springfield, Massachusetts.

Maya Lin, backed by a photo of the Vietnam Veterans Memorial, which she designed

Maya Lin

born 1959

Maya Lin was only 21 years old when she won a competition to design a Vietnam Veterans Memorial for Washington, D.C. The art world was stunned to learn that the designer whose work had been chosen from some 1,400 designs—many by professional architects, artists, and designers—was still in college. Maya's nontraditional design, combining art and architecture, brought her instant fame, praise, and controversy. Never giving up her unique vision, she has since designed other memorials, including a Civil Rights monument, as well as buildings, furniture, and sculpture. Her works reveal a flair for creativity and originality.

Artistic Spirit

The daughter of Chinese immigrants, Maya Ying Lin was born on October 5, 1959, in Athens, Ohio. Her parents met in the United States. Both had left China in the 1940s as the country was turning to Communism. Maya's father, Henry Huan Lin, became a professor of ceramics, while her mother, Julia Chang Lin, became a professor of literature. In time, Henry and Julia's interest in the arts rubbed off on both Maya and her brother, Tan, who became a poet and professor.

As Maya grew, art began to play a major role in her life. Eventually, it became the focus of her studies and career, but she pursued architecture as well. Many people focus on either art or architecture, but Maya combines the two fields. She also is interested in history

"A Mighty Stream"

"We will not be satisfied," said civil-rights leader Martin Luther King Jr., "until justice rolls down like waters and righteousness like a mighty stream."

Inspired by those words, Maya Lin used flowing water in her design for a Civil Rights Memorial in Montgomery, Alabama. Carved into a circle of black granite are the names of 40 people killed during the civil-rights struggle, as well as important events in civil-rights history. Water flows smoothly over the stone.

At the 1989 dedication of the memorial, Maya watched as visitors touched the names of loved ones who had been murdered. Some shed tears, which became part of the memorial's flow, linking the past to the present.

and the environment, both of which are reflected in her work.

While Maya was studying architecture at Yale University, students in one of her classes heard about the Vietnam Veterans Memorial competition and decided that each of them should enter a design. Some of the students, including Maya, visited Washington, D.C., to see the park where the memorial would stand. Looking carefully at the land, Maya thought that the memorial should become part of it, not overpower it.

She envisioned a *V*-shaped wall, made of polished black granite, that listed the names of the 58,000 U.S. men and women killed or listed as missing in action while serving in the Vietnam War. Maya wanted the names presented in chronological order, according to the date when each person died or was lost. In this way, she thought, the memorial would mark an era in time and be something that people could see and touch as a reminder of those who had been lost.

Maya did not want the memorial to make a political statement—the Vietnam War already had a long history of political upheaval. The years of U.S. military involvement in Vietnam (1964-1975) were a time of great debate and conflict in the U.S. Many Americans supported

U.S. efforts to stop the spread of Communism in that part of Asia. However, as the war continued and more and more U.S. troops were killed, a growing number of Americans opposed the war. Protesters staged antiwar marches and rallies, calling for peace. Unlike earlier wars, when troops were warmly welcomed home, returning Vietnam veterans were largely ignored, and many felt betrayed.

Monumental Achievements

The Vietnam Veterans Memorial design contest drew more than 1,400 entries. Contestants' names had been withheld from the judges, who were later surprised to learn that their talented winner was a young, female student. Maya and her design soon became controversial. Some people expressed concern about the design itself; some veterans said that it resembled a "scar in the earth." Some people disliked the black granite or the position of the wall. Some thought that a wall of

The Civil Rights Memorial in Montgomery, Alabama, designed by Maya Lin

21

> "*I imagined taking a knife and cutting into the earth, opening it up, an initial violence and pain that in time would heal. The grass would grow back, but the initial cut would remain a pure flat surface in the earth with a polished, mirrored surface.*"
> —Maya Lin,
> describing her design of the
> Vietnam Veterans
> Memorial

names would be too impersonal, and wanted a more traditional statue of human figures instead. Others opposed a memorial designed by a woman or by someone too young to remember the war. Still others complained about Maya's Asian heritage.

It was a difficult time for Maya. Although critics demanded changes to her nontraditional design, Maya held her ground: She believed that the names revealed the true depth of American losses in a way no statue could. Despite the controversy, the memorial was built and soon proved its detractors wrong. After it was unveiled in 1982, people flocked to see it; many were moved to tears. Today, "The Wall," as it is known, is visited by millions of people each year and has become one of the most respected monuments in the world.

After earning a master's degree in architecture, Maya opened an art studio in New York City, married, and had two children. Today, she is a popular architect-artist, creating buildings, furniture, sculptures, clocks, and other works. Among her most important achievements are the Civil Rights Memorial in Alabama; the Women's Table, honoring female students at Yale University; and the Langston Hughes Library in Clinton, Tennessee. Maya Lin's gift of imagination and artistic vision is highly regarded worldwide.

Life Lines

1959 Maya Lin is born in Athens, Ohio, on October 5.

1981 Maya's design for a Vietnam Veterans Memorial is chosen from among 1,400 entries; she graduates from Yale University.

1986 Maya receives a master's degree in architecture from Harvard University and establishes Maya Lin Studio in New York.

1989 The Civil Rights Memorial, designed by Maya Lin, is dedicated in Montgomery, Alabama.

1994 The documentary film *Maya Lin: A Strong Clear Vision* is released. It wins an Academy Award in 1995.

1998 Maya and her brother, Tan Lin, work together on a sculpture for the Cleveland Public Library.

2000 Maya's book *Boundaries* is published.

Leonardo da Vinci
born 1452 • died 1519

To call someone a "Renaissance man" or "Renaissance woman" is high praise indeed. It means that the person not only has a wide range of interests, he or she is also expert in several different fields. The original Renaissance man was Leonardo da Vinci *(VIN-chee)*. He lived during a period in European history known as the Renaissance *(ren-uh-SAHNTS)*, which means "rebirth." From the 14th century into the 17th, Europeans experienced a burst of new knowledge and creativity in literature, the arts, mathematics, and science. Even then, Leonardo was far ahead of everyone else.

Leonardo excelled in painting, sculpture, architecture, engineering, and science. He was a lifelong student, learning everything he could about music and math, geography and literature, nature and mechanics, and everything in between. His great gift was being able to balance a lively imagination—the ability to "see" what does not exist—with a solid understanding of the real world. According to an old saying, "He who has imagination without learning has wings but no feet." Leonardo da Vinci had both.

Earning His Wings

Leonardo was born in 1452, on an estate in the northern Italian town of Vinci. The boy was given an education worthy of a nobleman's son. When he reached the age of 15, his father sent him to the nearby city-state of Florence to become an apprentice to Andrea del Verrocchio, a well-known artist.

An artist's apprentice had a lot to learn, and Leonardo learned it all—and then some. He studied painting, sculpture, mechanical drawing, and human anatomy. (*Anatomy* is the detailed study of the various parts of the body, inside and out—what they look like and how they are put together.) His lifelong ability to draw anything, living or mechanical, in precise detail, came from his early training.

In 1482, the Duke of Milan hired Leonardo to be his official artist and engineer. (Milan—like Florence—was a city-state.) Today, we tend to treat the arts and the sciences as opposite disciplines; people usually focus their studies on one or the other. Leonardo did both: He executed beautiful paintings and sculptures, and organized grand festivals, while also designing and repairing buildings and machinery.

"Knowing How to See"

Leonardo was a great keeper of notebooks. In them, he made detailed notes about what he observed around him, writing backward. (Most people would need a mirror to read them.) For Leonardo, however, the drawings were more important than the words. He drew detailed

Leonardo's notebooks are filled with examples of a great imagination at work. Included among his sketches and notes are detailed pictures of devices drawn centuries before such things were actually built. His ideas came from absorbing all kinds of knowledge, looking at old ideas with a fresh eye, and combining ideas never combined before.

Sketches and notes (written backward) from Leonardo's notebooks: Opposite page—*a helicopterlike flying machine and a parachute.* Below—*human anatomy, a flying machine's wing, and a tank.*

sketches of all sorts of things, both those he had observed and those he imagined. Some of the most astonishing drawings were plans for objects that would not be invented, in usable form, until many centuries later. His detailed drawings of flying machines, for example, include plans for something remarkably similar to the helicopter, which was not successfully developed until the 20th century.

Leonardo believed that, no matter what one studied, sight was the most important of our five senses. He called it "knowing how to see." As he wrote in one of his notebooks, he would tell his art students: "I counsel [advise] you . . . to pause and look at the spots on walls, or the ashes in the fire, or the clouds, or mud, or other such places; you will make very wonderful discoveries in them, if you observe them rightly.

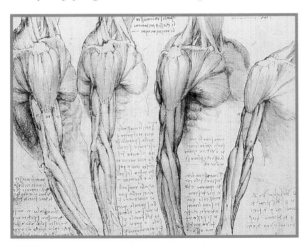

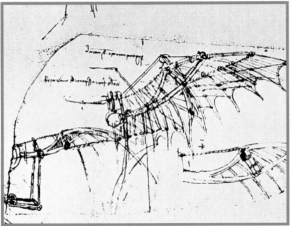

For the mind of the painter is stimulated by them to many new discoveries."

To look at something and see it clearly, Leonardo thought, was the best way to understand what it is and how it works. Once you know that, you are more likely to find a way to give shape to the things you imagine.

Of the many things Leonardo is famous for, two are paintings. One is *The Last Supper*. The other is considered the

Leonardo's La Gioconda

The *Mona Lisa*

Who is the dark-haired woman with the mysterious smile who gazes out of the world's most famous painting? Some experts think that she was the wife of a merchant named Francisco del Giocondo. (The painting's official title, *La Gioconda*, is a female form of the merchant's family name.)

The painting is so familiar, few people realize that it was revolutionary in its day—in technique (pose, colors, and background) and subject (a common person rather than a rich or important one).

Also, in capturing that mysterious smile, Leonardo revealed an inner life, giving the painting great impact. "[A] figure," he wrote, "is most praiseworthy that . . . best expresses the passions of the soul."

most famous painting in the world: *La Gioconda* (*JEE-uh-KAHN-duh*), better known as the *Mona Lisa*.

The breadth of Leonardo's imagination and abilities is impressive, not just for *his* time, but for all time. For any one person to be skilled in such a wide range of areas remains astonishing, as is the vast number and variety of objects he was able to draw, paint, describe, and design.

Leonardo spent his final years in the service of Francis I, the young king of France. The king, recognizing his employee's genius, honored Leonardo da Vinci by treating him as an esteemed guest—as the great man generations to come would know him to be.

Life Lines

1452   Leonardo is born on his father's family's estate at Vinci, near the city of Florence, Italy. (*Da Vinci* means "of Vinci.")

1467   Leonardo becomes an artist's apprentice in Florence, studying painting, sculpture, and mechanical drawing.

1482-1499   Leonardo works as an artist and engineer-in-residence to the Duke of Milan. He develops his skills and expands his knowledge of the sciences as well as art. During this time, he paints *The Last Supper*, one of his most famous paintings.

1500-1516   Except for 10 months traveling as a military engineer, Leonardo lives and works in Florence until 1506. While there, he paints the world-famous *La Gioconda* (the *Mona Lisa*). In 1506, he returns to Milan; from 1513 to 1516, he lives and works in Rome.

1519   On May 2, Leonardo dies in France, while working as the "first painter, architect, and mechanic of the king," Francis I.